Join the Winner's Circle!

7 Leading Authors and Business Experts Give You Proven Strategies and Tactics for Achieving Success

Copyright © 2021 1st Edition

Printed in the United States of America

ISBN Print Edition: 978-0-578-83744-4

3

Table of Contents

UPGRADE: WHO, HOW AND WHY TO CHOOSE!

by

Ron Hequet

Ron Hequet Consultant, Speaker, Coach is one of those rare individuals of who it is said to be a small business Entrepreneur and have the history to match.

Ron has successfully **owned and operated 8 businesses in 6 different industries** and has helped clients across the U.S. in over 20 different industries, and is considered...
'America's Achievement Coach'

Ron has written 5 books to date for the 3%'ers, and is a contributing author to the American Management Association, 'Leading & Learning E-Magazine', 'Affluent Magazine', 'The Advisor', and others.

'Unless you 'invest' in your own development, the time will never be right, you'll never be able to afford it and things will never turn around". That is a poverty mind-set usually held by those who are *too cheap or too lazy,* **the other 97%.**

3 FREE Bonus Gifts (a $997 value) go to:

www.FreeGiftFromRon.com

www.RonHequet.com

www.AmericasAchievementCoach.com

www.ProfitandCashFlowMarketing.com

"You are the average of the 5 people you most associate with."
— **Jim Rohn** American Entrepreneur and Author

Webster defines Upgrade in this way; *'to raise to a higher standard'*.

Have you ever gotten an upgrade, on an airline flight, a cruise, a resort stay, tickets to the opera, or similar activity? Most of us have or at least understand the idea.

All of the above examples give analogous results. We are moved to a different location, receive benefits others do not and we are surrounded by a different set of people.

Now before you get riled; I accept the fact that you and I may believe that those people are no better, and as God views it that is absolutely true.

Although all of the above examples have commonalities, let's use the airline upgrade, as it is probably most common.

When you receive an upgrade to first class, or comfort / premier seating, the following is a general overview of what takes place. You are now seated in a set-apart section of the airplane cabin from the rest of the passengers. First class seats are bigger, more comfortable and roomier. It has its own attendant(s) where beverages and a meal are a part of the fare. But, another important difference is usually the people flying in that section.

Over the years, I have had such seat partners as Terry Bradshaw (Hall-of-Fame Quarterback of the Pittsburg Steelers), Lee Trevino, (Professional Golfer and winner of every major event on the PGA tour),

Bill Curtis, (Chairman of the Southern Baptist Convention), and an assortment of CEO's, VP's, etc.

Now that the upgrade concept has been reviewed, let's apply **'Upgrade'** to **the 3% Winner's** reading this article.

Make a list of your current connections. A connection', as used here, is not people you *must* interact with. Current connections are simply defined as those people you go to lunch with, text, talk on your cell and go to the club, for coffee, movies and so on. As you think through and create this list, you *must* be honest with yourself about whom you truly spend time with whether or not it is business (so-called) or social. Your list should exclude family.

When you truly examine who you spend your time with, where you spend it and why you spend it, **97% will discover that your time, the most precious of all we possess, is not invested – but *spent*.**

Who to choose?

It is time to choose your connections. *Notice I said choose.* **Who you *spend* time with is a choice and so is who you *invest* your time with.**

Dr. David McClelland's study showed that whom you associate with, your "reference group", determined 95% of your success or failure.

In developing your 'upgrade' connections / new friend list(s), I suggest that you make an "A List" and a "B List". There can be a plethora of reasons why one or more of your choices is not at first accessible or may even at first reject your desire to connect. Notice I said, *at first*.

This is where most salespeople quit. They take a 'no' to their sales pitch personally. First, you're not selling anything, you're strategy is to **'upgrade'** your connections.

Also, your list(s) should be living, i.e. constantly being added to and / or modified as your career moves and new introductions appear. The entrepreneur that moves up is charting people you already know, people you want to know and then doing the preparative action required.

Having the answer to the following questions before starting to develop your list(s) will help clarify the best choices and who is qualified or who you desire to be on your list(s).

- ✓ Who are the most important players in your organization, in the competition's organization and / or in the industry?
  Note: *I don't care if you are currently working in the mail room.*
- ✓ It's imperative that you list the names of the decision makers and not the name of an organization, department or team…or
- ✓ Who is close to that person where I might develop that relationship first?

When developing your list(s), just brain storm without any filter, drawing from existing connections first, i.e.

1. Current co-workers
2. Previous co-workers
3. Past / present customers or clients
4. Fellow members of industry or other groups (if you don't belong, join!)
5. Networking groups (if you don't belong, join!)
6. School mates, etc.

Reading industry periodicals, newsletters or website postings and so on, will keep you up to date.

Achievers know it is not as important to be the best as it is to be the best connected.

How to choose?

Any idea or plan, such as we are developing here, cannot be achieved without confidence in your plan and in yourself. And, it is well established that **any plan that is not written down is not a plan, it is a wish**.

Why is it, that so few people have a plan? Research indicates that less than 3% of people have a personal plan.

Many years ago, Yale University did a study of a graduating class through a survey of many questions, one of which was, 'Have you set a clear and specific plan for your life?', and 'Have you written the plan down?'

They found that only 3% of the graduating class had specific goals and had written out a plan to achieve their objectives.

20 years later they interviewed the surviving class members and astonishingly discovered that **the 3% who had a definitive written plan, had a net worth greater than the remaining 97% all put together** – 20 years later.

This and other studies I have heard about confirm; it is consistent planners who are the achievers in business, and in life.

Do you want to depend on your memory for your plan?

When you meet someone, anyone, how you meet them, your opening impression and what they think of you after must not be left to happenstance.

I had the privilege of attending a private event where Joe Montana (Hall of Fame Quarterback for the San Francisco 49ers) was speaking. What most impressed me was his description of Coach Bill Walsh and the team's preparation. Bill developed a specific list of plays that would be called and in what order.

He called those plays regardless of the opponent's successful or failed response to the previous play. It was done on the practice field exactly that way, so the team was prepared for the carrying out of those plays without wondering about the next play being called because of what happened on the previous play. Their success is history and the point made of the importance of preparation.

So, before you attempt to reach out to a new connection, there is research to do. It will be extremely helpful if you know them, their history, their business, their achievements, what they feel passionate about and even their hobbies.

The preparation I am referring to is relatively easy. Who hasn't surfed the net? Googling someone of interest or checking them out on LinkedIn, Facebook or other social sites is mandatory and it's one of the easiest ways to "get to know" someone.

Review them on their organization's website. Have they written articles, were they the featured speaker at an event? The lower the career-rank of this person, the greater the difficulty in getting all the information that you would like. This also may be an indication that your target aim is too low.

Why to choose?

I have seen struggling people grabbing every business card they could get their hands on and attending every networking event.

The truth is that, those who have a record of contributing to profitability and have established connections inside their organization, outside their organization, inside their industry and outside their industry should be the first to connect with.

Just a few months ago, a person I know, Jack (not his real name) called me and wanted to meet for lunch or coffee. When we sat down, Jack recited a long list of achievements that he had accomplished for his current employer over the past 3 years and he also had prove-ups, with the calculated dollar benefit associated with all of them.

The non-conversant might think that without Jack the company would not have made any money or been out of business by now. Now I know Jack well enough that these accomplishments were real. He is not a braggart, nor does he exaggerate. His problem as he saw it was that there was not a position higher in the organization, Jack had hit the ceiling, just under the CEO and the Board of Directors, and his employer was not rewarding his accomplishments financially. I have consulted in his industry and Jack was correct, in that he was more valuable than what he was being paid.

Jack had also explored what others in a similar position at similar sized companies where being compensated. There was at least a 25% difference.

"Duh, have you had this same sort of presentation / conversation with your employer", I asked? Answer, "No." "Why not", I asked? "Well, I want to wait until I get through the audit." "Why", I asked? "Preparation for the audit is my responsibility and I don't want the distraction, in case the meeting doesn't go my way." "It's already not going your way", I said. "When is the audit", I asked? "About 3 months from now." I then asked, "After the meeting, what if your employer does not at least meet the market compensation for your position, what will you do, what are your options?" "I don't know I'll cross that bridge when I come to it."

I happen to know the results of the meeting with Jack and his employer. Let's just say that Jack has not gained any ground.

Jack is technically under-employed, and here are his options; continue to perform well and accept being underpaid, or **"Upgrade"**.

The percent of people with Bachelor degrees and MBA's without a job after graduation is growing every year, except for that 3% I keep referring to, for they have established an **"Upgrade"** of connections.

Now you must begin to build your list(s). **DO IT NOW!**

NOTES

You Are NOT in the (fill-in-the-blank) Business!
You Are in the Business of Marketing Your Business!

by

James Malinchak

Featured on ABC's Hit TV Show, *Secret Millionaire*

MEET JAMES MALINCHAK
The World's Leading Authority on Speaking
And The #1 Speaking Coach & Trainer

James Malinchak is recognized as one of the most requested, in-demand business and motivational keynote speakers and marketing consultants in the world. He was featured on the Hit ABC TV Show, **Secret Millionaire** and was **twice named National "College Speaker of the Year."**

James has delivered over 3,000+ presentations for corporations, associations, business groups, colleges, universities and youth organizations worldwide. James can speak for groups ranging from 20-30,000+.

As a **speaker marketing coach and consultant**, James has delivered 2,000+ Coaching Sessions and is the behind-the-scenes, go-to marketing advisor for many top speakers, authors, thought leaders, business professionals, celebrities, sports coaches, athletes and entrepreneurs and is recognized as "The World's #1 Big Money Speaker® Trainer and Coach!"

For more information & FREE Training, visit:

www.BigMoneySpeaker.com

Although today I am humbled to be one of the most requested and highest paid business and motivational speakers in America and have been featured on ABC TV's hit show *Secret Millionaire*, I didn't always experience the level of success that I'm blessed to have.

In my live event seminars, I always teach in a way that makes it easy for my audience to remember. When sharing with others, it's very important to keep things simple so people can easily comprehend your information.

There is one major lesson that has absolutely changed my business and life and that I know can change yours, as well.

You Are NOT in the (fill-in-the-blank) Business! You Are in the Business of Marketing Your Business!

I grew up in a small steel-mill town called Monessen, right outside Pittsburgh, Pennsylvania. There wasn't much optimism for life after the steel-town. Many never leave the town, which is totally fine. There's a specialness remaining in a town where you grew-up. However, I had some big dreams and goals that I wanted to pursue, which would require me leaving our town in order to pursue.

One day in junior high school, I was doubting myself and debating whether I could actually achieve my dreams and goals. Many thoughts of simply working in the mill after high school seemed to dominate my mind that day as my classmates and I were sitting in the school auditorium listening to a guest speaker.

The speaker shared a quote during his presentation that would forever change my life which was, "If you can dream it, you can do it.

That means YOU CAN do anything you want to do in your life if you always believe in yourself and never listen to those who tell you that you can't do something!"

WOW! It was as though a lightning bolt of inspiration immediately shot through my spirit. Although I didn't know it then, that bolt of inspiration would go on to become a driving force in my life to this day that would allow me to achieve many of those big dreams and goals,

Fast forward. Eventually I left my hometown and went to play college basketball at the University of Cincinnati, before transferring and graduating from the University of Hawaii at Hilo.

After college, I noticed a deep desire beginning to surface. I began thinking, *Wouldn't it be cool if I could help people the way that speaker back in junior high helped me? Wouldn't it be amazing if I could speak words that would help others to change their lives, exactly how that speaker spoke words that changed my life?*

In that very moment, I decided to become a paid speaker who got paid for doing what he loved, changing people's lives!

There was only one big problem. I didn't know what the heck to do in order to become a speaker who actually gets paid so I began asking people who were speaking who gave the impression they were successful. Everybody I asked in the speaking industry, the "so-called experts" (a term I use lightly) all told me the same things: "All you have to do is dream big, have passion, tell your story and simply be a messenger."

Looking back now, I realized there are two problems with that advice: (1) Most who were telling me that (and most I find today) don't actually make any real money speaking; and (2) None of that advice matters if you don't know the business-side of speaking which is how you really get highly, or what I now teach others, how you become a Big Money Speaker®!

When listening to these "so-called experts" (a term I use lightly), I was literally financially broke and forced to work in a video store making $7 an hour to help support myself, while trying to figure out why I was a failure, not being able to make it as a highly paid speaker.

At one point, I lived in a tiny apartment that was so bad; there were actually steel bars on the windows to make sure nobody would break-in. I even slept every night with softball bat just in case there was a break-in while I was sleeping (I'm not kidding).

Financially, it was getting tougher and tougher! Bills were coming in that I just couldn't cover. I tried everything to get paid make money speaking, but NOTHING seemed to work.

Self-doubt continuously ran through my mind, while I constantly felt bad about myself that the reason I wasn't making it as a highly paid speaker was because I wasn't dreaming big enough, wasn't passionate enough, didn't want to help people enough, didn't want to make a big enough difference in the world.

I can't even begin to tell you how discouraged I became. There were SO many times when I thought about "throwing in the towel" and walking away from pursuing my dream of getting highly paid to speak for sharing my message. I seemed to be just "spinning my wheels" and often felt like a complete failure!

I had no idea what to do! I was about to fall flat on my face and give-up, when one day...**The Major Turning Point!**

I was talking on the phone with a mentor, who's very successful in business and a multi-millionaire. While we were catching-up on things, I asked him why most of his businesses were successful. I figured he would say something about his extensive business knowledge or 30+ years of experience. But his answer shocked me...and became the "KEY" that was the "turning point" for my entire speaking business! He said,

"The reason is simple and is what I actually consider to be the key for anyone to succeed in ANY business, even the speaking business! The reason is because you shouldn't study and learn from people in the industry because most don't know how to market to attract business. Study and learn from top MARKETERS!"

"What? I'm not sure I follow you," I replied.

He continued, *"Nobody in ANY business could ever be successful if they don't know how to correctly market their products or services and get people to buy them. Just because someone is looked at as a top expert in your industry, doesn't mean they know how to market. So, why would you want to spend your time and possibly waste your money trying to study and learn from them? I'd rather just go right out and study and learn from top MARKETERS because they know how to do one thing better than anyone, MAKE MONEY FROM MARKETING!"*

WOW! Definitely NOT what I expected to hear! Immediately, a light bulb went off in my head! I knew this wealthy and successful mentor wouldn't have said that if he didn't mean it 100%.

What if I did the same!?! What if I studied and learned from top marketers and took what I learned and simply applied it to my speaking, writing, training, coaching and consulting business!?! Surely, it would work because principles are principles!

That was my aha moment. When I realized I'm not in the speaking business. I'm in the business of marketing my speaker services.

Realizing this and shifting my thinking, instantly changed my business and life! I mean, instantly!

I went from where I was, "spinning my wheels," feeling like a complete failure, ready to give-up and quit, to becoming one of America's most requested, in-demand speakers delivering over 3,000 presentations, conducting over 2,000 consultations, authoring over 20 books and doing over 5,000 media appearances, including being invited by ABC TV to be featured on their hit TV show, *Secret Millionaire.*

In addition, years ago I created my Big Money Speaker® training teaching others how to become Big Money Speakers® sharing their message, story and how-to advice, helping tens of thousands of people from over 40 countries.

Even today in my Big Money Speaker® training, I begin the entire training by saying, "I believe you already have passion, mission and desire. You want to be a speaker because you want to make a difference in the lives of others. So we're not going to spend time discussing any part of that. Instead, we're going to spend all of our training on teaching you what I wish someone would have taught me when I was starting out: *How I could help others while getting highly paid for sharing my message, story and how-to advice. In essence, you're going to learn how to become a Big Money Speaker®!* What's amazing is people begin loudly applauding every single time because that is exactly what they desire!

So what does this mean for you? It's simple. Please understand there are two sides to every business. One side is your passion, mission and desire to help others. And the second side called the business, especially marketing. Most people fail in business because they don't realize they should be spending the majority of their time focused on marketing.

It's very simple. If people don't know about you and the value you bring to the marketplace, then they can't buy from you. Anybody who doesn't want to believe this truth won't be in business very long.

Marketing is not something you do to people. It's not manipulation. It's something you do for people by letting them know you and your great value exists. So it's ok to market! You're not a bad person if you market because if what you do does what I call AME (Adds Value, Makes a Difference and Enriches Lives) why wouldn't you want everyone to know about it? Marketing isn't trickery and manipulation. You're simply letting people know that you exist so tell everybody and remember:

You are NOT in the (fill-in-the-blank) business!

You are in the business of marketing your business!

*_NOTE:_ Because you are reading this, you are entitled to _receive a FREE Copy of James' Best-Selling Book_, Millionaire Success Secrets: 33 Unique Ways to Think & Act Like A Millionaire Top Achiever!

Receive Your FREE Hard-Cover Book (a FREE $25 value) **_Plus 3 FREE Bonus Training Videos_** (a FREE $997 value) by visiting:

www.MillionaireFreeBook.com

NOTES

What Unicorns Do...
Or the 4 Most Important
Things to Focus on
To Scale Your Business

by

Patty DeDominic

Patty DeDominic: an award winning business coach and entrepreneur and coach to Super Achievers in Business.

Patty ran her own successful 600 person business for 27 years before becoming a business coach in 2007. She has helped numerous business owners grow 10X and even 100X.

She was entered into the Women Business Owners Hall of Fame over 20 years ago, was honored by US Presidents for her community leadership and is the former chairman of the US Foundation for SCORE.org

If you would like a complimentary business audit, to review the 5 pillars of your business and identify your leadership opportunities, I am happy to offer this to you free of charge.

Visit our blog for more tips including Getting Unstuck or Getting past that first Ten Million in sales.

https://www.dedominic.com/what-unicorns-do

Simply write to me to request your Complimentary consult/ business audit.

I wanted to get your attention when I use the term "Unicorns". Webster's defines this as not only as a mythical animal but something that is highly desirable and difficult to find or obtain. You might be lucky enough to have worked for one, often a start-up that is wildly ambitious and attracts top talent and investors to eventually grow to sell for over One Billion Dollars or with sales exceeding a billion a year.

Just a few years back I was privileged to join by acquisition, a company that had been started by an entrepreneur much like me. I watched as that company catapulted past $100 million in sales, then past $500 million and via added acquisitions and a pumped-up sales team, eventually grew sales to over $1.8 billion in the final year I was associated with them.

Where are you in your growth plan? Do you want to get twice your current size? To serve one hundred more customers? To employ 500 people? No matter what your goal, you can benefit by the focus that Unicorns must have to make their ambitious goals.

Not everyone wants to grow their company to a billion or even One Hundred Million in sales or valuation, but there are some practices that these mega successful businesses deploy that you can also use to grow your business 2 x's, 5 x's and 10 times its current size in as little as a year or two. You do not have to take decades like I did to finally hit your first $50 million in sales.

As a 28-year-old founder and entrepreneur, I never thought I could grow a business 100 times over but was able to do that in my career in the executive search and staffing industries in 27 years.

After I sold my business in 2006, I learned more secrets not only of my industry but of the mergers and acquisitions field. I also discovered the "secrets" that are not *really secrets*, just smart business practices of mega successful companies.

First…the small guys often stay small because they are trying to do every job themselves. We often take great pride in being essential and in making every dollar work as if it were ten. This is needed for startups with few customers and less than optimal working capital. We pull ourselves up by our bootstraps and proudly proclaim that we are self-made millionaires. Self-made yes, but mega corporations and great successes, even by icons like Steve Jobs, Elon Musk and Mark Zuckerberg needed teams. You need a great team.

Unicorn tip # 1 -   Surround yourself with the best people you can possibly afford.
Utilize the best talent for advisors, contractors, and employees. Your net worth and the speed of your success are highly enhanced by surrounding yourself with as many A-Team members you can get. Think world championship sports teams…we are all winners, yet for the winning sports team we choose players with promise and proven track record.

For your staff – hire for promise and <u>previous accomplishments</u>. Hiring Interns and on-the-job trainees may look like money saving tricks, but they really suck up your resources. Like most entrepreneurs, they just don't know or have enough experience to pull our high growth business through the tough times.

Let me tell you about the unicorn that bought my companies PDQ Careers and CT Engineering. They had a founder, who had been replaced years earlier by a professional (former Wall Street CFO Type) chief executive officer.

They had a team which was always on the hunt for new acquisitions because their growth and business strategy dictated growing to hundreds of millions of sales in contract staffing. Once we had executed our letter of intent for them to purchase my company, they put a specialized team in place to do the evaluations and the reviews needed for the due diligence process.

A special admin, perhaps even a paralegal, assembled all the documents and reviewed our contracts, our leases and any employee compensation agreements. They wanted to be sure they were buying a business with proven revenues, profits and income that would continue long past the time the founder (me) and employees would be around.

Each role and function had a champion and a key person responsible for "owning" a certain set of tasks and deadlines. Always setting smart goals with project owners and deadlines was one of their secrets to getting through piles of legal paperwork and the exhausting process of inspecting a multimillion dollar acquisition.

Unicorn tip # 2 - Focus is one of the most powerful "free" tools at your disposal. Remember to focus all your resources and much energy on the most important goals and the best people as they will give you the highest return on investment ROI.
After I sold my company, I could easily see why they had grown, and I had stayed at under $100 million.

I had been dividing myself into a hundred different pieces, trying to be a mom, a wife, a good community volunteer, a CEO and business owner, a board member for the Chamber of Commerce, and yes, when I had time, I might work on my fitness or might look for acquisitions. I did not use the power of focus like the big boys did. My mistake that cost me ten years of growth.

What is your business, right now? Can it use more of your Focus? What issues, if you put all your energy and best thinkers and advisors on a problem or opportunity, could come true this year? Choose carefully, and you can make those bigger goals come true. Put your best people on the biggest opportunities. Put your problem solvers on solutions needed to shore up any weak spots that could blindside you later. Protect your Achilles heel!

Unicorn tip # 3 - Your time is your most valuable resource. We all have 7 days in a week, 24 hours in a day and 1,440 minutes in every day.
How do you leverage and focus YOUR most precious asset? Let me ask that again: How do you leverage and focus **your time**? Often entrepreneurs are busy battling the urgent, consumed and conflicted because they battle many recurring problems. Are you getting the best terms? Are you paying too much for supplies, inventory or for credit? Many entrepreneurs make this mistake.

John was a construction contractor who had lines of credit and usually financed his supplies and materials purchases on his credit cards. Getting new cards and small credit lines were easy; the banks always sent him tempting offers. We analyzed his finances, sales, costs, and profits as part of what I do when I bring on a new coaching client. Guess what we found?

He had paid over $75,000 in high interest charges in the past year and his interest rates with those benign-looking easy cash cards were costing him over 30% interest and penalties for any payment that was even one day late.

Interest rates vary and this was a few years ago, but we went to his bank and got a consolidation loan at 5% interest. The money saved by restructuring his debt was enough to open a second location in a much higher end neighborhood and that new store immediately doubled its average sales.

Remember, everything is related, and one process improvement can bring on the need for more. But if you shore up the major leaks in your profits, you can add millions to your bottom line even if sales do not increase exponentially at first. Make a regular schedule to upgrade your procedures.

Unicorn tip # 4 – Your <u>Systems</u> will make you much more effective and efficient.   Create a culture of refining systems, upgrading processes and make sure all of these get documented so that the next person in the role has a running start.
Even pilots use check lists. You need them too and your people need them more. You can get every process out of people's heads and onto a resource that is used by your whole team.

Automate and delete outdated processes. Create a calendar item to review your processes at least twice each year. Put your best "librarian/efficiency expert" on this system and keep it up to date.

To recap some of the top secrets of How Unicorns Do it:

A. Surround yourself and your team with the best you can afford. Cheap help is way too expensive if you are serious about growing your business and building a business you may one day sell or pass on to the management team or your kids.

B. If it is important to do, then put FOCUS to work on it.   Focus is like magic and if you try to spread yourself too thin, and if *"everything is a priority"* then *NOTHING* is a priority.   Know your priorities and focus only on them until they are successfully accomplished.

C. Leverage your time and watch the benefits to you grow.   Doing fewer, better actions and working with fewer better people will pay off.   You can get 80% of your accomplishments done by less than 20% of your actions.   Understand the difference and teach your people to manage their time well too.

D. Create Systems for continuous improvement. If it needs to get done, then it needs to get documented. Upgrade and automate as many of your processes in selling, managing, servicing clients, and running your business.   Reduce dependency on any one person and make sure you have done overlap and cross training.   You want your organization to continue to grow even if you lost your top sales or office people.   Even if the founder retires, you want to build a system-driven organization, which is enhanced by people and innovation, not a people-dependent company.

What's Trust Got to Do With It?

by

James L. Capra

James L. Capra is an author, professional speaker and currently the CEO and Founder of the Front Line Leadership Group located in North Texas. With his unique experience of over three decades as a warrior and public servant, Mr. Capra shares real world examples and uplifting stories of what it takes to develop outstanding leaders who pursue excellence in their professional and personal lives.

He is the author of *Leadership at the Front Line*: *Lessons Learned about Loving, Leading and Legacy from a Warrior and Public Servant*; a children's book; *The Eagle and the Seagulls: A Wisdom Story for Children and Adults.*

His third book co-authored with his wife Shelly, *Raising Courageous Children in a Cowardly Culture: The Battle for the Hearts and Minds of our Children*, details the challenges of raising children in culture devoid of moral principles.

Mr. Capra holds a Bachelor of Science from Marist College and a Masters of Education from Seton Hall University. He has been married to his wife Shelly for over 38 years and they are the proud parents of six outstanding children, most who have taken up lives as public servants. He can be contacted at...

www.frontlineleadershipgroup.com

Over the course of my nearly four decades as a public servant both in the uniformed military services and as a federal agent, I have witnessed a number of leaders ranging from the truly incompetent to the truly incredible. While there are a number of characteristics that embody great leaders, I submit that the number one characteristic found in most outstanding leaders is their intrinsic desire to truly care about and learn to love those they serve. These leaders understand that they need to make an emotional connection with organizational members because they understand that developing positive relationships often results in producing the fruit of trust in the lives of their people and in the organization as a whole. Conversely, those organizations that are run by fear and intimidation are typically doomed to fail in their pursuit of growth and production and those leaders who practice the same leave a legacy of chaos, mistrust and anger within the organization.

Often, when I am asked about the underlying problems in business, in national security issues or in personal endeavors, it seems that the major issue comes down to a failure of trust and pursuing success instead of pursuing excellence. You see you can cheat and be successful, you can lie and be successful, and you can implement immoral and/or unsafe business practices and be successful; but only for a limited time. Ultimately, pursuing success at all costs, or pursuing personal success at the cost of others will result in a failed business, a failed organization and a failed personal relationship.

It is becoming more apparent that we are a nation that has a trust crisis; that is, it would seem that everywhere we turn, trust appears to be on the decline. Our trust in government, our trust in Wall Street, our trust in organizations, our trust in our clergy and our trust in each other continues to wane. In an article written by Stephen Covey, many years ago, he wrote, *trust in our culture at large, is significantly lower than a generation ago.* This has been proven out again and again; not much has changed as we are daily barraged by the growing number of legal battles played out in our state, local and federal courts because of the lack of trust between organizations and people. That is, we have become a society focused on contracts as the primary means to protect our interests and we have forgotten what it is to have a covenant relationship between organizations and each other.

For the most part, we no longer pursue covenant relationships. The term covenant means "a coming together"; a commitment that binds two parties together and carries with it the concept of cleaving to one another. Covenants are the fruit of a faithful relationship of trust; covenant partners take responsibility for their actions; covenant partners nurture their relationship. There was a time when trust was a social expectation between two or more people, organizations or entities. However, in the past decade or so, it seems that as a culture in business, in government or in personal endeavors, we no longer expect a relationship of trust, rather we expect deception and are constantly on the lookout for actions and deeds that will support our expectation of deception at work, at home or in our business markets. If we are constantly looking for deceit in any relationship, just think of the burden and costs of the emotional, physical and mental stress when our relationships are based upon the notion that one party will ultimately be deceived.

Although implementing contractual obligations are necessary in the global business environment, it appears that many organizations resort to contractual agreements as a strategy to develop loyalty from business partners and employees. Contracts are based on protection and mistrust. Yet we find that agreements by legal negotiation, and enforcement by legal processes and accounting argumentation is costly, causes bad blood and reduces the moral obligation of each party to live up to an agreement; it causes delay and essentially destroys relationships. There must be a better way to succeed in the global business environment!

Although many leaders believe that trust is difficult to measure, there is without a doubt a tangible benefit to high trust in any organization. Studies conducted by a multitude of firms over the past decade have shown time and time again that high trust companies outperform companies of low trust. The Watson Wyatt survey showed that high trust companies outperform low trust companies by nearly 300%.
Let that sink in for a moment; *300%*...as a CEO, COO or any organizational leader would you be willing to allocate resources, time and energy into something that would increase your organization's performance, manufacturing and/or profitability by 300%? And here is the kicker, it's not something you have to go out and physically purchase; an

additional widget, building or computer software program; it is however, something that you have at your disposal right now, which is, do you have the courage to consider how to implement a shared philosophy of trust within your organization?

The reality is that many CEOs and organizational leaders think of trust as a soft, sort of nice to have virtue and do not believe that trust is directly connected to their organizations bottom line. Covey rightly pointed out that trust affects two measurable outcomes – speed and cost. Therefore, when trust goes down, speed goes down and costs go up. Conversely, when trust goes up, speed goes up and costs go down. No matter how you slice it, a lack of trust costs us in tangible ways in every facet of society.

Consider the reasoning behind the governments' continual use of legislation to initiate regulatory compliance laws that are directly related to the loss of trust in the business sector. For instance, years ago, Sarbanes-Oxley was passed in response to the major scandals of Enron, World-Com and other corporate disasters. Although this intrusive government regulation may have helped maintain trust in the public market, those executives subject to this regulation understand the amount of time it takes to comply with the law as well as the added cost of compliance. According to a study, the implementation of just one section of Sarbanes-Oxley cost businesses 35 billion dollars which exceeds the original estimates done by the SEC by 28 times. And that was just Sarbanes-Oxley; the estimates of the cost of complying with federal rules and regulations in the US alone often exceed 1 trillion dollars. And of course, those costs are ultimately passed on to other stakeholders, partners and consumers. Compliance regulations often come as a lack of trust between the government and private business. Instead of trust, quite often legislators at multiple levels believe that it is necessary to prevent deceit…and it is expensive!!

I have been told that I simply don't understand that these regulatory policies are a necessity in a global business environment to ensure due diligence and to protect large multi-national companies from failing and or deceiving other companies for profit. But then how do we explain Berkshire Hathaway CEO Warren Buffet's acquisition of

McLane Distribution – a 23-billion-dollar company from Wal-Mart? According to Covey, a deal of this size involving public companies would typically take several months to complete and cost several million dollars in due diligence. But because both parties operated with high trust, this deal was made with one two-hour meeting and a handshake. In less than a month, it was completed. Buffett wrote in his annual report: "we did no due diligence.' We knew everything would be exactly as Wal-Mart said it would be-and it was."

Yes, but that's Warren Buffet you say, you can't compare Warrant Buffet to another organization; and I say why not, maybe we should consider that besides being good at business, Mr. Buffet excels at and understands the "speed of trust!" Maybe, just maybe, business leaders such as Mr. Buffet recognized a long time ago that trust, that so called soft, sort of nice to have virtue, does indeed have a tangible return on such an investment. More importantly, based on Mr. Buffett's statement in his annual report, it is clear that he went into this transaction with the expectation of trust, not deceit.

It should worry us as a people and as business leaders that 40% of people polled say they have little or no trust in corporate America, with 47% feeling that way about Fortune 500 CEOs. That same survey asked respondents to identify a single phrase from a list that would engender the most trust in a company. They chose "ethical business practices," and "sound moral compass." Trust starts at the top by a leader who recognizes the importance of developing a relationship with his team, with his staff, with his/her workforce. Trust doesn't start when you issue a policy or a SOP…trust can be viewed and is actionable.

The ability to engender trust to employees, stakeholders, shareholders and partners is a necessary competency for any leader who strives for excellence in his walk.

As a competency, engendering trust is something that leaders can learn and become good at IF…they are willing to lead from the heart. That is, from my tenure as a leader in government, I have witnessed organizational cultures grow, thrive and be successful, when leaders first learn and demonstrate care and love for those they are entrusted to lead, which includes employees, partners and stakeholders.

Character and competence for any leader is a must. Leaders, who are dedicated to treating people right (The Golden Rule), consistently deliver superior value and retain outstanding employees. Employees who recognize that they are valued and cared for by those that lead them, often provide superior service and value which generates pride and a sense of purpose among employees that can be tangible. Ahh, the question for us all is simply, How…how do we get to a culture of trust, how do we develop a trust climate, how do we implement trust across the organization, where do we/I start?? You start at the top, not at the middle, not with HR, not at the bottom and you certainly don't start by telling your work force, *hey, trust me!!!*

Let me start with 3 principles; People, Purpose and Passion. You begin to build a foundation of trust by developing a moral position that people, as does the organization, have a purpose. Our people not only have a purpose in the organization, but have a moral purpose in life. The best leaders recognize the importance of developing employees both professionally and personally with passion. This is done by a leader's ability to develop relationship in order to make trust a goal that is communicated and matters to all levels within an organization.

If you want to become a great leader, if you want to make a difference in your team, unit, your organization, if you want to make a difference in your leadership walk, if you want to develop a culture of trust in your organization…you need to learn how to love the men and women you are entrusted to serve! I call it Leading from the Heart at the Front Line! This is not a quiver in your liver or everybody gets a hug. This is about really caring about those you serve and ensuring accountability. You see, I believe that your desire as a leader should be for those you are entrusted to lead; your heart's desire should be for them to grow professionally and personally. This is not about everybody gets a hug…this is about a willingness, a conscious effort to care about those that are entrusted to you.

The bottom line is not money, not profit, not mission; the bottom line is people and when those people are led by leaders who care about them, organizations thrive, employees excel and grow, and missions and goals are achieved in their respective markets.

TRUST STARTS WITH DEVELOPING RELATIONSHIPS

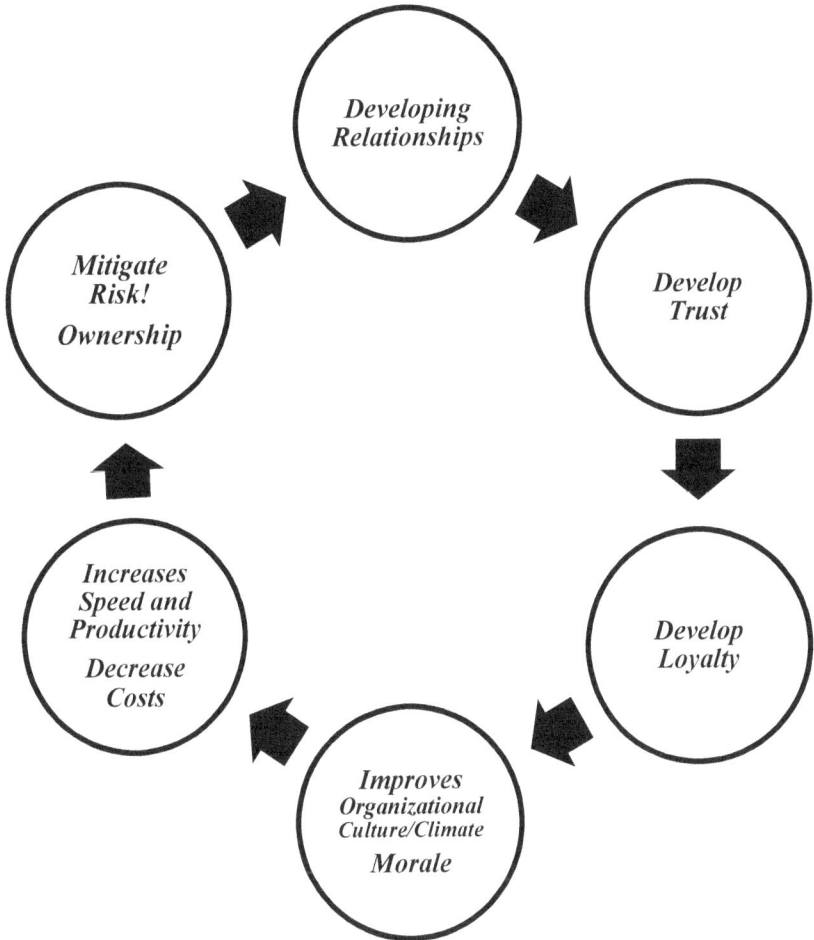

Developing Relationships

Develop Trust

Mitigate Risk!

Ownership

Develop Loyalty

Increases Speed and Productivity

Decrease Costs

Improves Organizational Culture/Climate

Morale

The Benefits of Moving from a Push to a Pull System

by

Henry F. Camp

Henry F. Camp - After earning a BA in Mathematics at the University of Virginia, Camp taught for several years before joining Shippers Solutions, where he designed and programmed his own ERP system to improve the company's operational effectiveness. After five years, he bought the company and still owns it, having grown sales tenfold. www.ssco.pro

A $4 billion customer implored Mr. Camp to manage their $70 million raw material inventories in 4 different countries. New software was created and deployed. Within months, five warehouses in four countries all demonstrated 6σ inventory accuracy. More importantly, the client's shortages disappeared, which had previously delayed about a third of planned production schedules. Moreover, inventory required dropped 70%. This spin off became IDEA, LLC, of which Henry owns the majority. www.ideallc.com

IDEA expanded scope, delivering supply chain consulting using replenishment software based on constraints theory. By this time, Henry formed a personal relationship with Eli Goldratt author of *The Goal*. A major client was **Adidas**, who used IDEA's Elucidate software to double their same-store sales without increased inventory or expense. Henry became recognized as a worldwide authority in supply chains.

Camp shifted to buying companies instead of consulting. He raised money to establish TOC Equity Partners which acquired and substantially improved several companies, using TOC and his business operational expertise. This first crop of acquisitions has either been sold or is being positioned for sale at dramatic profits.

 Camp published his second book in 2019 titled *Throughput Economics,* with constraints theory experts Eli Schragenheim and Rocco Surace. The book expands TOC Throughput Accounting, showing how to apply a simple holistic approach in many different business cases. *Throughput Economics* helps companies improve quickly and significantly. As its ideas are more broadly adopted, future difficult economic shifts will be made easier, enhancing the world economy. He is currently establishing The Aviation Protection Fund, which will support commercial airlines.

Manufacturers, distributors, and retailers are forced to choose the approach they hope will make them the most profit. Is it producing and making goods available ...

- ... to forecasts of expected consumer demand, or
- ... by reacting to what consumers already bought?

Conventionally, companies use the former approach. In what we term a "Push system," *product availability is based on forecasts*. Companies forecast to feel confident that the goods they buy, sometimes many months in advance, will both be used and not run out unexpectedly soon. In the Push world, decision points occur at every reorder. How much should be purchased at a time? In other words, how often is it necessary to buy each item? In attempting to prevent stock-outs and protect sales/production, buyers end up with fewer inventory turns than they wish.

Pushing inventory downstream through the links of the supply chain is a natural response to the desire to reduce over-investment in inventory, as well as to record sales today rather than later.

In contrast, a "Pull system" *controls the flow of products by automatically adjusting inventory levels according to actual consumption.* Pull systems simply respond to what consumers buy. A Pull system manages time buffers of inventory for each item. These buffers act as shock absorbers, which are compressed as inventory is consumed until replenishment can occur. For each consumption, an equivalent order is placed. This approach lends itself to automatic electronic processing. Replenishments are frequent, in the smallest economical batches. Decision points in Pull systems are triggered only occasionally, to resize buffers, when on-hand inventory levels consistently correspond to too little or too much protection time.

Push

Supply chain issues like high carrying costs, discounting, disposals, missed sales, weak customer loyalty, shortages, high debt loads, inventory disposals, emergency shipments, rescheduled production and attenuated profits all stem from three common root causes.

1. Inaccurate forecasts
2. Long replenishment times and
3. Variability in both demand and replenishment times

Perhaps, the nastiest of the three causes of problems in Push environments is that forecasts are always wrong. Despite billions spent annually in the US for the best computers and most sophisticated software, actual demand varies from forecasts. Forecasting does not make the end consumer react more rationally or predictably. When it comes down to it a forecast is only a guess, no matter how sophisticated its algorithm. Wrong guesses mean excess investment and lower profits, due to missed sales.

Pull

Pulling goods through a supply chain is analogous to (but more straightforward than) adapting the Toyota Production system (TPS) – the progenitor of Lean – to manufacturing. Toyota's management has used TPS for over 60 years to earn remarkable and consistent profits, amass a cash hoard and drive its market capitalization higher than those of Volkswagen, Daimler, Ford and GM combined. Perhaps such an approach to supply chains should be considered, even though it seems counterintuitive to choose to behave reactively rather than proactively.

Each link in a Pull supply chain tries to improve replenishment speed and orders smaller batches more frequently. Pull systems use demand data to drive both replenishment and production.

Only immediately expected customer requirements are drawn from the protective inventories upstream.

By acting on actual demand, statistical variations are damped rather than magnified; steadying on-hand inventory levels at every stocking location. There is a very nice consequence of less fluctuation in on-hand levels. The lower limits of the on-hand fluctuations are similar to those in a Push system, fixed by the need to hold prudent safety stocks. However, in Pull systems there is less variation on the high side, resulting in significantly lower average inventory. See Figure 1, below.

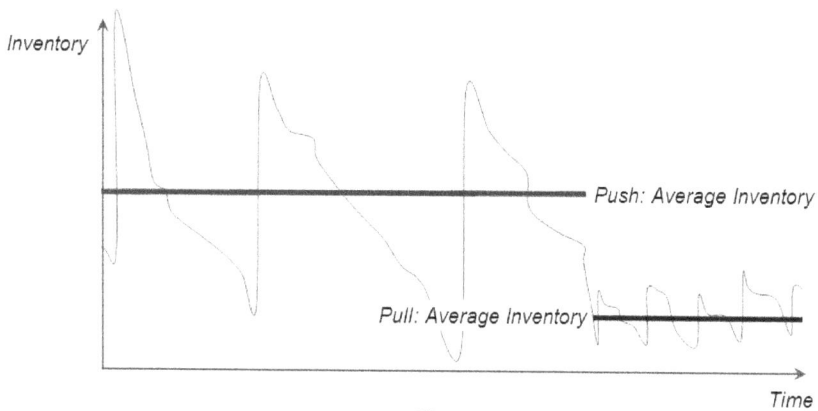

Figure 1

There is another effect on the supply chain as a whole. Since goods only flow downstream to cover immediate need, the preponderance of the inventory remains further up the supply chain, closer to the source.

The demand variations of a store are greater than that of a region, because the region's sales are the aggregated sales of all its stores. The same thing is true at a central production plant as compared to the regions it serves. The more the aggregation, the better statistical highs and lows offset each other. Okay, so what? Here's what: variability is proportionally less at the places where demand is aggregated, and safety stocks are sized to protect against variability.

So, safety stocks are proportionally less when they are closer to the source, where Pull supply chains hold most of their inventory.

Consequently, there is much less inventory in a Pull supply chain for two reasons: first, less variability naturally results in lower average inventory (again this effect is shown in Figure 1 above) and, second, overall safety stocks are smaller due to where inventories are predominantly held.

Furthermore, shortages are reduced by Pulling. Because there is a constant flow of goods inbound, there is a quicker response to short term changes in demand, improving availability. To address longer term changes, buffer management matches stock of each product at each location to changes in replenishment time and demand, keeping buffers matched, even though the situation continually changes.

In summary, one-to-one ordering with frequent replenishment, combined with buffer management liberates companies that adopt Pull from reliance on expensive and unreliable forecasts. Implementing this approach increases a company's revenues without increasing operating expenses and reduces investment in inventory. The results are stunning improvements in financial performance.

Effects of Push and Pull on Retail

Push systems are particularly devastating to retailers. They accept the massive inventory push from their suppliers to drive local improvements such as these:

1. They choose long replenishment times in return for lower costs to facilitate the highest possible markups.

2. In many retail environments, they cannot replenish within a season, so they accept everything they hope to sell in advance of each season.

3. They broaden their product selection to attract customers to compete with other shops that sell similar products.

4. They fear missing sales, and so, buy to optimistic forecasts.

5. They must organize outlets or discount heavily to sell off the surpluses, undermining their brand.

Consumer tastes change and more and more manufacturers roll out new products to address consumer demand. Slow moving products sit on the shelves, blocking newer products and those in higher demand.

Frequently, a product that is in abundance at one retail location is short in another. Not having the right products on shelves causes customers to walk out of stores when they don't find what they are looking for. Ultimately, surplus inventory is pushed on consumers. Retailers run promotions and offer discounts in order to move the mountains of inventory. Those lovely full-price markups seldom survive the effects of discounting, shrinkage, disposals and fire sales. The sum of these effects in addition to lost sales exerts enormous negative financial pressures on retailers. When management is unaware of the alternative, this pain is stoically accepted as normal.

Virtually all retailers end up with much more inventory than they need to cover immediate consumption. Despite high margins, retailers are financially fragile. Think Sears, Best Buy, Neiman Marcus, J.C. Penny, J. Crew, Aldo, Pier 1, Toys R Us, Radio Shack and Brooks Brothers. Too much inventory kills.

In a Pull system, using readily available point-of-sale (POS) data as inputs, shortages can be reduced by an order of magnitude due to the quick response nature of these flow systems. More product is always about to arrive, especially when inventories are low. Customers find what they need, when they need it, where they need it, and complete a purchase more often. Customer loyalty and upbeat word-of-mouth increase. Patrons are less likely to resort to a competitor. New sales are the result – sales that require no additional operating expense.

The indirect impacts of lower inventories on sales are not less important than the reduction of shortages. Lower inventory means less shelf space required per item. The resulting unused shelf space and surplus cash allow the retailer to stock a wider variety of items. Sales increase significantly from the same physical space. With lower inventories per item, retailers need fewer markdowns and promotions, firming gross margins.

There are many fewer slow-moving items clogging shelves at the expense of better sellers and recently introduced products. In a Pull scenario, there is also less exposure to costly shrinkage and obsolescence. Yes, profits increase due to lower carrying costs, but more significant financial improvement comes from higher sales revenue and margins – dramatic improvements in the retailer's net profit return on their inventory investment.

Effects of Push and Pull on Distributors

Traditionally, inventory is pushed onto the distributor who is encouraged to purchase large orders from the manufacturer. Incentives for these large orders are quantity discounts offered by the manufacturer and lower transportation rates per unit.

Because cash is tied up due to high levels of inventory, distributors are limited in what products they can afford to stock.

The longer inventory stays in a distributor's warehouse, the higher the risk of declining prices and obsolescence. Both significantly lower profits (although often not until many accounting periods later, when the causal actions are forgotten and the people who took those actions have left, making it difficult to avoid repetition). A distributor must turn their inventory to get the most from their investment. So, they use lower pricing and expensive incentives to force products on customers. Naturally, the need to turn inventory takes priority over being in harmony with end-user demand and changing trends.

In a proper Pull system, distributors share point of sale data with their manufacturers, helping the manufacturers smooth the load on their plants, decreasing production response time. Distributors can commit to their suppliers to take large quantities over time but in smaller, more frequent shipments. Since they are replenished more often and more quickly, distributors hold less of each SKU.

The distributor concentrates on, and even sells the advantages of, rapidly replenishing its customers. When customers get products quickly and reliably without paying a premium, there is no reason for them not to hold considerably less of each item. Without a glut of inventory clogging their operations, they respond to their customers more quickly, increasing their sales and profits, while cash is freed up. Their higher volume also benefits the distributor.

With less investment, distributors grow faster and offer a broader variety of products. In return for their much better service, they need not discount as often or as deeply and they earn more business from their Push competition.

Effects of Push and Pull on Manufacturing

Conventionally, manufacturers produce large batches of product in an attempt to increase productivity, save setup time, and cut production costs. This practice creates excess inventory of some products while delaying production of other products in high demand.

Accrual accounting says a manufacturer's profits are driven by shipments. To appear stronger, they force inventory into the distribution channel as quickly as possible, packing the supply chain.

In Push supply chains, different links communicate through orders. If a manufacturer has overloaded the downstream supply chain with product, there will be a delay before better than expected demand is communicated to the manufacturer in the form of new orders. Imagine what happens. About the time heavy orders arrive, the manufacturer has a production schedule which includes everything except the new high-flying items. The resultant wait for a production slot temporarily starves both distribution and retail channels. There results a feast and famine cycle, which may not resolve itself before consumers, fall in love with something new.

With a Pull system, communication of demand is in the form of actual daily end-user purchases, which are quite steady at the manufacturer, the point of highest aggregation. Without surges of orders, manufacturing capacity designated to handle peaks is available to produce the consistently higher sales produced by a Pull supply chain.

When production is planned based on actual sales, it stops the wasteful practice of buying raw materials and running plants just to produce surplus inventory which clogs up the supply chain. Plants that convert to Pull produce smaller, more frequent batches, dramatically enhancing availability. Since each item is produced more often, there are fewer emergencies and faster reaction to changes in consumer demand. The result is fewer stock-outs, increased sales, less obsolescence and fewer disposals.

Pricing to the next link down the supply chain is based on the (increased) total consumption rate, rather than order size. Pricing in this fashion eliminates the last incentive to overload the plant, leaving protective capacity to produce the higher level of demand that results from switching from Push to Pull. Sales are increased by the win-win nature of the new policy. Throughout the supply chain inventory turns and profits increase.

In Summary
The Pull system described here helps all links in a supply chain overcome the frustrating and damaging side effects of Push systems in wide use today. To fully realize sales, service, and profit potential, companies must realize how constantly forcing inventory to the next link in the supply chain before it is needed actually limits their results.

It can be said that *"unless the end consumer has bought, no one in the supply chain has sold."* Making the transition is a challenge. You don't need to buy special software or hardware, what is required is much more difficult: adopting a new way of thinking and behaving!

NOTES

How to Prepare Yourself for (Almost) Anything

by

Cheryl Williams

Cheryl Williams is a freelance copywriter, copy editor, and proofreader with over 25 years of experience as a fundraising professional.

She's written and edited newspaper articles, grants, fundraising copy, and newsletter copy and currently is working on a children's book series.

If you need a consistent voice and fresh customer-centered content, she offers blog writing and original content creation.

You can contact her at...

https://www.linkedin.com/in/cherylwilliamscopywriting/.

Is it possible to be ready for anything? Realistically, the answer is no. However, with a measure of preparation, we can minimize the confusion and unwanted outcomes when the unexpected disrupts our world.

Not long ago, the unexpected rocked my world. I discovered that I had been hacked. The hack compromised my computer, smartphone, passwords, and email addresses.

It started with an unsolicited request via email to verify a login attempt to my Health Savings account. Because I believed it was a one-off, I didn't give it much thought. Next, I noticed a couple of low dollar charges on my credit card that I hadn't initiated. A day later, I discovered that someone in a different state had ordered food using another one of my credit cards. That alone was enough to jar me out of denial. Still, the occurrences kept escalating.

On the day I got paid, someone moved money from my savings to my checking account, I assume to make it easier to withdraw. I had checked the account on my smartphone that morning and everything looked good. I reasoned that there was no way I could have *accidentally* moved money from one account to another. However, the pièce de résistance came during my frenzied rush to secure my other accounts. I discovered that the hacker had initiated a sell order of stock from my retirement account.

As an influx of evidence uncovered the extent of the cyberattack, I started scrambling to cover my assets. I installed a password manager and updated the easy-to-guess passwords that I had used over and over. I switched to multi-factor authentication.

I closed and reopened my bank accounts, locked my credit files and invested in an internet security service to monitor suspicious activity on the dark web.

The cyber onslaught continued for nearly a week and it was exhausting! I lost sleep, peace of mind, and confidence in the "system." Given the increasing sophistication of cyber hacks, I don't know if anybody is truly safe, but in my case, I'm grateful that it's now a lot harder for hackers to exploit my cyber weaknesses.

My mistake...I got sloppy. The best defense truly is a good offense. I hadn't used the knowledge and resources available to me to avoid the attack. I learned a hard lesson about being careless and a valuable lesson about being prepared. Not just with my finances, but in my daily life. It's been said, "If you stay ready, you don't have to get ready. I've found that to be true. Here a few tips I've used to stay nimble and prepared and reduce the chances of being caught off guard.

1. Live a Healthy Lifestyle

That includes both mind and body. Don't allow negative thoughts to overwhelm you or simply stick in your head like that song you heard yesterday. It prevents you from giving your full focus to the good things happening right now in your life. In addition, it may cause you to miss an answer or an opportunity. Likewise, when your body is sluggish due to poor eating habits, inactivity, or lack of sleep, it affects your judgement and ability to make wise decisions. If you want to maintain a sharp and responsive mind, and a body that will allow you seize the moment, take care of yourself.

2. Get organized

Being disorganized wastes both time and money. Believe me I know. When you can't find something that you've spent hours or days looking for, you just buy another one. That's how I ended up with four Black and Decker cordless drills...the same drill. When I finally started organizing and decluttering, I discovered that I had been buying the same things repeatedly because I had forgotten that I had them.

Even my groceries were not immune. Hiding in the back of my kitchen cabinets were tarnished cans of tomato paste, full bottles of Worchester sauce and exotic grain mixes that seemed exciting at the time I bought them. Some of the food was so old, excuse me...vintage, that I considered selling it on eBay. Here's a thought. Simplify by donating or selling reusable items. Put things together that belong together. Check your inventory before you buy more stuff. Avoid drama and people that contribute to confusion. Start by taking small steps, and you'll realize that you can put both your time and money to better use.

3. Save Money

If you can, start saving money at an early age or as soon as you are able, you'll discover that your financial stability gives you the freedom to make smart choices. Being strapped for money can put a strain on your relationships and a place a lock on your dreams. If you develop the patience and discipline to delay present desires for future gain, you'll reap a harvest when you don't give up.

4. Stay Informed

Ahhh...ignorance is bliss. Sometimes it feels good to ignore events that don't directly affect us. We think that because we've never experienced something, it's less relevant and unworthy of our attention. Instead, I believe our humanity connects us all. We all eat. We all sleep.

We all cry. We all bleed. When you refuse to know for yourself, it's easy to get caught up in the doctrines of people who may not have your best interest at heart.

Read, listen to a credible news source, learn something on YouTube, and make a new friend. Put yourself out there. Then become a doer and not just a hearer. I doubt that life will ever stop throwing you curve balls. But when one comes your way, you'll be prepared to stand your ground and hit it out of the park.

5. Don't Do Anything Stupid
I know that sounds harsh, but stupid actions can have devastating consequences. Have you ever watched videos of adults who attempted daredevil feats of chance and then failed to make it?

Owwww! I feel their pain. But they're happy because they proved some random point, right? Being prepared includes using wisdom to make right choices and having the courage to walk away from wrong ones.

6. Handle Your Business
If you have a job, own a business, are raising a family, going to school, caring for a loved one, or simply working on yourself, do what you do with excellence. Be the person who makes a worthwhile contribution to others rather than the one who feels like everybody owes you something. You'll earn the respect of your family, peers, and colleagues and your generosity will not go unnoticed or unrewarded.

7. Check Yourself
Mistakes are going to happen because we're not perfect. I'd like to think that most people are eager to rectify the situation and hope that it never happens again.

However, I've known people who don't seem concerned about how the mistakes they make affect the recipients. They have a loose attitude about the problem they caused as if detached from the responsibility. They don't seem to understand or care about the inconvenience their negligence caused. Usually these mistakes result from the lack of checks and balances and are wholly preventable.

If this sounds like you, then you can prepare for success by making a commitment to double check the work you do. Make a list of the steps you need to follow and check the off as you complete them. You'll be less likely to miss a critical process and more likely to add value to your friends, family, employer, and others by gaining their trust as you become more reliable.

8. Rein in Your Emotions

It's hard to make a rational decision when your emotions are raging with fear, anger, loneliness, jealousy or even passion. Think about it. When you fall in love, the object of your affection can do no wrong. That person is the smartest, kindest, most beautiful and perfect person you know. They have no faults...until you have an argument or break up. Then you start seeing flaws you didn't notice before. The flaws were always there, but your emotions concealed the truth.

Controlling your emotions can help you see through the clouds of your desires and give you a more authentic picture of who you really are and what you really need.

9. Don't Take It Personally

A lot experiences that you believe are directed toward you are not really about you.

Sometimes by proximity, association, or coincidence, you'll get caught up in other people's messes, dilemmas, accidents, lies, and if you're lucky, their good fortune. If you believe life is against you and people are out to get you, you could end up manifesting a self-fulfilling prophecy. In other words, what you say and think could become your reality.

If you're harboring hurt or disappointment because of something someone said or did, it helps to try to understand the why behind the action. Even if you never figure out why, learn to shake it off and don't give it another thought.

10. Let it Go

Sometimes, in order to keep the peace, avoid arguments and move forward quickly, I take the responsibility for a situation gone wrong. It's fruitless to spend time trying to reason with people who believe they didn't contribute to the misunderstanding.

If I'm able to diffuse a situation by saying something like, "My bad," then that's what I'll do. Don't get me wrong. I'm never going to confess to someone else's crime. However, I prefer to keep things moving rather than being stalled by accusations, anger, and hurt feelings. Ain't nobody got time for that!

Petty arguments and disagreements can clutter your mind with what you should have done, what you're going to do, what you should have said and what you're going to say. Your non-stop thoughts about the situation guarantee that you'll never be free of it.

If you expect the situation to end badly, then it probably will. Let it go. Break the chains of this type of oppression by practicing forgiveness. The sooner you move on, the sooner you can have what you really want.

11. Be Ready to Pivot

Change is hard on some people, especially constant and unexpected change. I work in that type of environment. Mandates abruptly trickle down through managerial layers, and by the time they get to me, they are watered-down, unclear, and urgent. While I don't necessarily like this game, I've learned how to play it. I'm convinced that my contribution is vital to the implementation of the company's goals.

When the time and resources you're expected to work with are limited because you and others didn't or couldn't prepare, be adaptable and look for the workaround. In the words of Martin Luther King, Jr., "If you can't fly then run, if you can't run then walk, if you can't walk then crawl, but whatever you do you have to keep moving forward."

NOTES

The Greatest Motivational Tool

by

Rod Olson

Rod Olson or Coach O' is a catalyst and Coaches' coach known for his ability to help high performing leaders and executive teams see things others don't see and find their 'sweet spot' as they lead and motivate others in the 21st century.

He is the founder of the Coaches of Excellence Institute and the Coach O Consulting Group. Rod is also the author of three highly acclaimed leadership fables: The <u>Legacy Builder,</u> <u>Wisdom Lunch Warrior</u> and <u>Greatest Motivational Tool</u>.

After nearly 20 years as a college football coach, Rod has spent the last decade plus, working with elite teams and organizations while teaching, coaching, and mentoring some of the top coaches and leaders in our country.

He is a nationally recognized speaker and leadership consultant specializing in high level leadership coaching and culture development.

Rod has clients in the corporate sector, professional and collegiate sports and in our United States military elite special forces.

If you want more information on Rod, how to purchase his books, executive coaching & team consulting or have him speak to your leaders he can be reached at: <u>RodOlson.org</u>

"Rod, we want you to keep teaching and facilitating workshops for our coaches and leaders, but I really want you to increase your 1 on 1 meeting this year. The staff workshops are important, but I believe your 1 on 1 meeting are a competitive separator."

This quote came from one of the executives of an organization I've been working with the past few years. In the last month and a half, I have had nearly seventy-five 1 on 1 meeting with business executives, professional and or college coaches and military leaders.

Before I tell you why I believe the 1 on 1 meeting is one of, if not the most powerful motivator of people in today's world, let's look at the top 2 complaints I hear from today's players and employees and then from their coaches and leaders.

THE TOP 2 COMPLAINTS FROM 21st CENTURY PLAYERS AND EMPLOYEES

1. "I just don't feel like they (their coach or boss) care about me as a person."
2. "I wish they would give me clearer expectations. It seems like they always wait until the end of the quarter or season to tell me how I was not performing the way they wanted me to."

TOP 2 COMPLAINTS OF 21st Century EXECs and COACHES

1. "We couldn't have been more clear in our expectations, why aren't they performing at the level we need them to?"
2. "We have parties, we do team building activities, yet we still have people and teams underperforming and complaining that they don't feel engaged. I want to know, how can we get in front of this?"

I want to share with you why it is so important for you to be doing timely and consistent 1 on 1 meeting with your players and or staff. Secondly, I will give you a simple format or formula you can use to ensure a productive and positive meeting.

WHY do I need to be doing 1 on 1 meeting more often?

Harvard Business review has done recent studies and articles on the ineffectiveness of one-time yearly reviews. In fact, many successful companies and firms are actually doing away with them in lieu of the consistent 1 on 1 meeting throughout the year. Also, **clarity of purpose is essential to high performance.**

Everyone always says you can't over communicate your mission, vision and values enough. Well, you can't over communicate your expectations enough with the people you lead and that include our children. Lastly, if people feel like they are valued and that you are growing them both professionally and personally, they will rarely leave for another job or team. You want to develop great people...meet with them 1 on 1. You want to keep great players...meet with them 1 on 1. But to accomplish the latter, these meetings must be done correctly, so let's discuss how.

HOW do I run an effective 1 on 1 meeting and how often?
The first question that needs to be answered is how often should I execute 1 on 1 meeting?

SPORT COACHES: Over the last decade, I have found the most optimal frequency of meetings between players and coaches is a minimum of 3 meetings when in-season and 1 per month in the off-season (with weekly texts woven in).

IN-SEASON 1 ON 1 MEETING SCHEDULE:

#1- Execute 3 Weeks into the season (this way, you and the player can evaluate: performance, possible roles, and their personal life; i.e., "How is life going for you personally now that you are roughly a month in?"

#2-Execute just after the Mid-Point of the season and discuss the same things as above, with more emphasis on the role they are finding themselves in or you want them to pursue.

#3-Execute 1 Week prior to the conference tournament, playoffs or final game. *Note this is not an exit interview. At this point, you will discuss everything listed in the meetings above and their role in the upcoming games as it may have changed due to injury etc.

BUSINESS LEADERS/EXECS: Over the last decade, I have found the most optimal frequency of 1 on 1 meeting between executives and team members is a minimum of one time per month and additional quarterly reviews.

Coaching Points: I would perform both on-site and off-site 1 on 1's with my team members. At least 1 time quarterly I would take the team member off site, perhaps for a short coffee meeting as a change-up. **Quote to remember as a business leader or Executive: "No one should ever be surprised that they are being let go or fired."**

A SIMPLE FORMAT FOR YOUR 1 ON 1 MEETING

1. Give them the 3 P's at the start of every meeting: Purpose, Process and Payoff

People don't like to be ambushed, tell them the purpose of the meeting is to give them clarity on everything and help them grow professionally and personally.

2. The PROCESS: Discuss what they are doing well. Next, their One Big Thing (OBT) to improve and lastly, the plan of HOW you will be helping them succeed.

People need to feel safe, secure and significant so hunt what they are doing well first and remind them of why you recruited or hired them. Secondly, give them only 1 thing (OBT) to work on, not 3 or even 2. Lastly, they must feel like you are here to help them and are in it with them. After all, you are either coaching them or letting their lack of improvement happen.

3. The PAYOFF: Ask them to tell you what their 1-TakeAway for themselves was from this meeting. Your people should walk away from this meeting with great clarity and you need to make sure they are taking away the "Right" thing...Remember high CLARITY creates high performance.

The biggest mistake I see coaches and execs make in their 1 on 1 meetings is to not make the team member state, verbally (to them), what they are expected to do moving forward. Or worse, the team member states the wrong thing or many things, and the leader doesn't bring them back to the main thing or their one big thing.

When done correctly, 1 on 1 meetings can be one of the most powerful motivation tools you can utilize. So why don't we do them? Perhaps the #1 reason is time and a lack of understanding of how to control the content and outcome of the meetings.

Yes, people are messy and at times require high maintenance, but in the 21st century you and I can't afford not to stay out in front of things. You simply can't wait until the end of the year or season. Your players and people want clarity and relationship.

You don't need to be their buddy to do a 1 on 1 meeting; you just need to be their coach and mentor. There is much more to write on this topic on the art of the 1 on 1 meeting, but hopefully this gives you enough information to help you move forward in helping your people be the best they can be.

Make it a great day and be a Legacy Builder!

NOTES

NOTES

www.ingramcontent.com/pod-product-compliance
Lightning Source LLC
Chambersburg PA
CBHW071442210326
41597CB00020B/3909